I0199329

Finn J.D. John:
<u>CURRICULUM VITAE</u>
2017 Edition

Finn J.D. John

CURRICULUM VITAE

2017 Edition

By **FINN J.D. JOHN**

Instructor, New Media Communications
Oregon State University
Room 30-J Snell Hall
Corvallis, OR 97331

541.357.2222

finn.john@oregonstate.edu

For full contact info see Page 35

Pulp-Lit
PRODUCTIONS
Corvallis, Oregon

Copyright ©2017 by Finn J.D. John.
All rights reserved.

First edition: Hardcover
ISBN: 978-1-63591-001-8

Other editions:
E-book (EPUB format), ISBN 978-1-63591-903-5: Download at [ofor.us/903]
E-book (Kindle MOBI), ISBN 978-1-63591-904-2: Download at [ofor.us/904]
Interactive PDF, ISBN 978-1-63591-906-6: Download at [ofor.us/906]
Traditional printable PDF, ISBN 978-1-63591-908-0: Download at [ofor.us/908]

Pulp-Lit Productions
Corvallis, Oregon

http://pulp-lit.com

CONTENTS:

INTRODUCTION.

My name, as you will have gathered, is Finn John, and this slim volume contains my curriculum vitae — the sum and summary of my professional and creative life as of January 2017. What follows is a brief biographical summary, just to put the statistics into proper context.

I have spent most of my life in the newspaper business. Ten years ago, though, sensing trouble ahead for my industry, I went back to graduate school, earned a master's degree, and parlayed that into a new career as a college instructor of new media, in a program that puts a great deal of emphasis on media entrepreneurship.

This position more or less forced me to spend a lot of my spare time learning everything I could about the way stories are told and information is shared in a rapidly changing media environment. I was fortunate in that upon admission to graduate school in late 2008, I had launched a weekly self-syndicated newspaper column, *Offbeat Oregon History*, with an eye toward providing small community newspapers with "semi-local" content that could be used to fill unexpected gaps. Now, two years after its launch, this franchise offered me real-world content in the form of more than 100 archive columns, with which I could explore new multimedia and trans-media channels and methods of storytelling. As a result, over the following years, *Offbeat Oregon History* expanded from a small independent syndication service into one of the most well-known and widely used public-history franchises in the state.

Insights gleaned in the process of building *Offbeat Oregon History* were instrumental in the establishment, in 2014, of Pulp-Lit Productions, a trans-media publishing company that specializes in omnibus collections of classic works of "pulp fiction" and focuses particularly on audiobook production. Insights gleaned in the operations of Pulp-Lit Productions, in turn, have been put to work in classes at Oregon State University, including, most recently, a two-part Special Topics studio class titled "Trans-Media Publishing in Genre Fiction." In preparation for that class, I created a 70,000-word novel in the romantic suspense genre (*The Trouble Deep*, under the *nom de plume* of "J.J. Davitt"), which will be used as a demonstration piece for the various trans-media self-publishing opportunities available to novelists today.

My most recent project is an alternate-reality storytelling experiment called the "Friedrich Wilhelm von Junzt Library of Forgotten Worlds," which also functions as an outreach tool for some of the more obscure titles published by Pulp-Lit Productions. Its core canon asset is a weekly podcast reading of a selected weird-fiction short story from one of the less-well-known authors of the early 1900s, reading from out-of-print collections of the short stories of authors such as Algernon Blackwood and Arthur Machen; it also has its own publishing imprint under the Pulp-Lit aegis, F.W. von Junzt Bibliothekspreße, under which it publishes reprints of those old collections in hardcover, softcover, e-book, and audiobook form.

About this CV:

The curriculum vitae you hold in your hands is, of course, somewhat unconventional. It is the result of applying a spirit of media entrepreneurship to the somewhat tired medium of the traditional vita. As such, it includes some features designed to enhance its usefulness as a tool of communication.

1. It's a trans-media publication. You are reading the hardcover book version of my vita. If you find it more convenient, you can also obtain it in e-book form (as a free Kindle .MOBI or .EPUB file through direct download, or through the Kindle store for a 99-cent fee); as an interactive PDF, with live outbound links — or, of course, as the usual and familiar stapled-together stack of letter-size paper. All these versions can be downloaded or accessed from the shortened URLs listed on the copyright page of this book (page iv).

2. It's an index, not a summary. Lengthy though it is, a print-media curriculum vitae like

this can't do much more than name-check the various creative works it references. That's why, in the formats that make it possible to do so, I have included as many hyperlinks as possible (and reasonable), so that you can, with one or two clicks and in less than two minutes, be directly reviewing any asset that's mentioned in this vita.

Of course, that cannot be done in the printed version. Instead, therefore, I have made shortened URLs using my own short-URL domain, http://ofor.us ("**Off**beat **Or**egon"), and inserted them, in **boldface type** between [square brackets], everywhere a hyperlink would go if this were an electronic text.

Thank you!

Finally, thank you very much for taking time to review my curriculum vitae. I hope that you find something interesting here, and that perhaps we can work together on interesting, enlightening, and mutually beneficial projects sometime soon.

Cordially,

Finn J.D. John

Finn J.D. John:
CURRICULUM VITAE

2017 Edition

I

EDUCATION *and* EMPLOYMENT.

Education:

Master of Science, Literary Nonfiction (Journalism), University of Oregon   June 2010
- Lead professor: Lauren Kessler
- Terminal project: *America's Most Hated Hero: How Herbert Hoover Saved an Entire Nation from Starving During the First World War.*

Bachelor of Arts, English Literature (honors), University of Oregon   June 1991

Employment:

Instructor, Oregon State University, New Media Communications   2010–Present
One-year renewing teaching appointment at 4 classes per term (no research component). [Faculty profile: **ofor.us/osu**]

Principal Creative (owner), Pulp-Lit Productions   2014–Present
Pulp-Lit is a trans-media publishing house with special emphasis on audiobook production, with offices in Corvallis. [**pulp-lit.com**]

Graduate Teaching Fellow, University of Oregon School of Journalism and Communication   2008–2010

Newspaper Journalist, Lee Enterprises and Black Press   2000–2009
- Reporter, copy editor, columnist, *Corvallis Gazette-Times* and *Albany Democrat-Herald* (2002–2004, 2006–2009);
- Editor-in-chief, *The Springfield News* (2004–2006);
- Editor-in-chief, Cottage Grove Sentinel (2000–2002);
- Editor, *The (San Juan) Islands' Sounder* (2006).

Correspondent, The New York Post   2003–2004

Editor and publisher (owner), Travelin' Magazine (Eugene, Ore.)   1998–2000

Associate Publisher, The Real Estate Book of Eugene/Springfield   1995–1998

Newspaper journalist, Gannett Co.   1991–1994
- Reporter, *Silverton Appeal-Tribune, Mt. Angel News, Stayton Mail,* and *Salem Statesman Journal*

II

TEACHING *and* ADVISING.

Curriculum Development:

NMC 303 Visual Media Writing:
Developed as new Writing Intensive Curriculum class for fall 2017 (in process).

NMC 499 Special Topics: Trans-Media Publishing in Genre Fiction, Part I:
Studio production class developed for winter 2017. [Syllabus: **ofor.us/499a**]

NMC 499 Special Topics: Trans-Media Publishing in Genre Fiction, Part II:
Studio production class developed for spring 2017. [Syllabus: **ofor.us/499b**]

NMC 100 New Media and Culture (with Dr. Joshua Reeves):
Large-lecture baccalaureate-core class developed for winter 2017. [Syllabus: **ofor.us/100**]

NMC 499 Creating a Fictional World:
Four-week intensive summer course developed in spring 2014. [Syllabus: **ofor.us/499**]

NMC 498 Capstone: Building a Trans-Media Franchise:
Four-week intensive summer course developed in spring 2014. [Syllabus: **ofor.us/498**]

NMC 399 Media Spin Detecting:
Developed as a new class in spring 2013. [Syllabus: **ofor.us/399**]

NMC 321 History of Broadcasting:
Developed as a new class in spring 2012. [Syllabus: **ofor.us/321**]

NMC 101 Intro to New Media:
Revamped at department head's request in winter 2011. [Syllabus: **ofor.us/101**]

NMC 301 Writing for the Media Professional:
> Took over existing syllabus in Fall 2010; revamped to better match departmental goals in winter 2012 following discussions with other faculty. [Syllabus: **ofor.us/301**]

Advising and Student Collaboration:

OSU Novelists Club:
> Helped a group of students form this group in spring 2015. Currently serve as faculty adviser to the group.

Kristopher Jerome:
> Worked with Kris in a two-term independent study to help him develop and launch a trans-media franchise centered around his 110,000-word novel [**ofor.us/dt01**], winter and spring 2015.

Nathan McLoughlain:
> Collaborated with Dr. Shawna Kelly in two-term independent study with Nathan as he developed a journal article, subsequently published in Well Played, winter and spring 2014 [**ofor.us/wellplayd**].

Joanne Davaz:
> Served as Honors College thesis adviser for Jodie's senior thesis project, spring 2015.

Gabriel Bennett:
> Worked with Gabe in one term of independent study helping him develop a nonfiction book project, winter 2013.

Teaching:

Credit courses, Oregon State University:
> Winter 2017:
> - NMC 100 New Media and Culture: 100 students;
> - NMC 301 Writing for the Media Professional: 20 students;
> - NMC 399 Media Spin Detecting: 30 students
> - NMC 499 Special Topics: Trans-Media Publishing in Genre Fiction: 20 students.
>
> Fall 2016:
> - NMC 301 Writing for the Media Professional: 19 students;
> - NMC 301 Writing for the Media Professional: 19 students;
> - NMC 321 History of Broadcasting: 40 students;
> - NMC 399 Special Topics: Media Spin Detecting: 28 students.
>
> Summer 2016:
> - NMC 301 Writing for the Media Professional: 17 students;
> - NMC 498 Capstone: Franchise Building: 16 students;
> - NMC 499 Special Topics: Creating a Fictional World: 12 students.

Spring 2016:
- NMC 301 Writing for the Media Professional: 20 students;
- NMC 301 Writing for the Media Professional: 21 students;
- NMC 321 History of Broadcasting: 35 students;
- NMC 399 Special Topics: Media Spin Detecting: 30 students.

Winter 2016:
- NMC 101 Intro to New Media: 52 students;
- NMC 301 Writing for the Media Professional: 19 students;
- NMC 321 History of Broadcasting: 38 students;
- NMC 399 Special Topics: Media Spin Detecting: 25 students.

Fall 2015:
- NMC 301 Writing for the Media Professional: 16 students;
- NMC 301 Writing for the Media Professional: 19 students;
- NMC 320 History of Telecommunications: 41 students;
- NMC 399 Media Spin Detecting: 27 students.

Summer 2015:
- NMC 301 Writing for the Media Professional: 11 students;
- NMC 498 Capstone: Franchise Building: 25 students;
- NMC 499 Creating a Fictional World: 10 students.

Spring 2015:
- NMC 101 Intro to New Media: 37 students;
- NMC 301 Writing for the Media Professional: 20 students;
- NMC 301 Writing for the Media Professional: 18 students;
- NMC 321 History of Broadcasting: 35 students;
- NMC 399 Media Spin Detecting: 15 students.

Winter 2015:
- NMC 101 Intro to New Media: 50 students;
- NMC 301 Writing for the Media Professional: 20 students
- NMC 321 History of Broadcasting: 40 students;
- NMC 399 Media Spin Detecting: 23 students.

Fall 2014:
- NMC 301 Writing for the Media Professional: 20 students;
- NMC 301 Writing for the Media Professional: 18 students;
- NMC 320 History of Telecommunications: 40 students.

Summer 2014:
- NMC 301 Writing for the Media Professional: 6 students;
- NMC 498 Capstone: Franchise Building: 18 students;
- NMC 499 Creating a Fictional World: 10 students.

Spring 2014:
- NMC 301 Writing for the Media Professional: 20 students;
- NMC 301 Writing for the Media Professional: 18 students;
- NMC 321 History of Broadcasting: 25 students;
- NMC 399 Media Spin Detecting: 36 students.

Teaching (continued):

Winter 2014:
- NMC 101 Intro to New Media: 50 students;
- NMC 301 Writing for the Media Professional: 21 students;
- NMC 321 History of Broadcasting: 41 students;
- NMC 399 Media Spin Detecting: 27 students.

Fall 2013:
- NMC 301 Writing for the Media Professional: 21 students;
- NMC 301 Writing for the Media Professional: 21 students;
- NMC 320 History of Telecommunications: 69 students;
- NMC 399 Media Spin Detecting: 8 students.

Summer 2013:
- NMC 301 Writing for the Media Professional: 6 students;
- NMC 399 Media Spin Detecting: 11 students.

Spring 2013:
- NMC 101 Intro to New Media: 40 students;
- NMC 101 Intro to New Media: 40 students;
- NMC 301 Writing for the Media Professional: 22 students;
- NMC 321 History of Broadcasting: 54 students.

Winter 2013:
- NMC 101 Intro to New Media: 51 students;
- NMC 101 Intro to New Media: 49 students;
- NMC 101 Intro to New Media: 51 students;
- NMC 301 Writing for the Media Professional: 22 students;
- NMC 321 History of Broadcasting: 36 students.

Fall 2012:
- NMC 101 Intro to New Media: 49 students;
- NMC 101 Intro to New Media: 51 students;
- NMC 301 Writing for the Media Professional: 21 students;
- NMC 320 History of Telecommunications: 71 students.

Summer 2012:
- NMC 101 Intro to New Media: 21 students.

Spring 2012:
- NMC 101 Intro to New Media: 49 students;
- NMC 101 Intro to New Media: 47 students;
- NMC 301 Writing for the Media Professional: 21 students;
- NMC 320 History of Telecommunications: 66 students.

Winter 2012:
- NMC 101 Intro to New Media: 44 students;
- NMC 301 Writing for the Media Professional: 22 students.

Fall 2011:
- NMC 101 Intro to New Media: 67 students;
- NMC 301 Writing for the Media Professional: 19 students;
- NMC 320 History of Telecommunications: 75 students.

Spring 2011:
- NMC 101 Intro to New Media: 79 students;
- NMC 301 Writing for the Media Professional: 26 students;
- NMC 320 History of Telecommunications: 71 students.

Winter 2011:
- NMC 101 Intro to New Media: 59 students;
- NMC 301 Writing for the Media Professional: 26 students.

Fall 2010:
- NMC 301 Writing for the Media Professional: 26 students.

Credit courses, University of Oregon (graduate fellowship):

Spring 2010:
- J 461/561 Copy Editing (with Gerald Sass): 18 students.

Winter 2010:
- J 461/561 Copy Editing (with John Russial): 20 students.

Fall 2009:
- J 203 Writing for the Media (with John Russial): 35 students.

Spring 2009:
- J 202 Information Gathering (with Tracy Miller): 40 students.

Winter 2009:
- J 202 Information Gathering (with Tracy Miller): 31 students.

Fall 2008:
- J 202 Information Gathering (with Mark Blaine): 29 students.

Student evaluations:

Average student evaluations (out of 6 possible):
- 2016: 5.02
- 2015: 4.94
- 2014: 5.06
- 2013: 4.76
- 2012: 4.94
- 2011: 4.70

III

SCHOLARSHIP *and* CREATIVE ACTIVITY.

Research interests:
- Trans-media franchise creation and management as a venue for creative expression;
- Sociological and literary analysis of vintage pulp fiction and its genre-fiction equivalents
- Book and audiobook publishing and production;
- Oregon history.

Publications, Academic (peer-reviewed):

Articles:
- McLachlain, N.S., Kelly, S.K., and John, F.J.D. "An unlikely partnership: Problem-solving with Lara Croft," Proceedings of the Games+Learning+Society 11th annual conference. Pittsburg, PA: Carnegie Mellon University ETC Press, 2015 [ofor.us/gls11].
- McLachlain, N.S., Kelly, S.K., and John, F.J.D. "Actions speak louder than hypersexualized pixels: A partnership with Lara Croft," Well Played Journal: A journal on video games, value and meaning, v.5 n.3. Pittsburg, PA: ETC Press, 2015 [ofor.us/wellplayd].

Conference presentations:
- McLachlain, N.S., Kelly, S.K., and John, F.J.D. "An unlikely partnership: Problem-solving with Lara Croft." Poster session presented at Games+Learning+Society 11th Annual Conference, Madison, WI, July 7-10, 2015.

Publications, Trade Press:

Books:

- Howard, Robert E., and John, Finn J.D. *Robert E. Howard's Conan the Barbarian: The Complete Omnibus Collection (annotated)*. Pulp-Lit Productions, 2017. Hardcover, paperback, e-book, audiobook [**ofor.us/p27**].
- Blackwood, Algernon. *The Listener and Other Stories*. Edited by Finn J.D. John. 1922. Pulp-Lit Productions, 2016. Hardcover, paperback, e-book, audiobook [**ofor.us/p60**].
- Davitt, J.J. [Finn J.D. John]. *Trouble Deep*. Bankshott Books, 2016. Hardcover, paperback, e-book, audiobook [**ofor.us/p80**].
- Smith, E.E. *The Skylark of Space: The Original 1928 Edition*. Edited by Finn J.D. John. 1928. Pulp-Lit Productions, 2016. Hardcover, paperback, e-book, audiobook [**ofor.us/ p26**].
- Lovecraft, H.P. *Supernatural Horror in Literature*. Edited by Finn J.D. John. 1925. Pulp-Lit Productions, 2016. Hardcover, paperback, e-book, audiobook [**ofor.us/p29**].
- Lovecraft, H.P., and John, Finn J.D. *Fungi from Yuggoth: The Sonnet Cycle, Contextualized with a Selection of Other Lovecraft Poems*. Pulp-Lit Productions, 2016. Hardcover, paperback, e-book, audiobook [**ofor.us/p28**].
- Lovecraft, H.P., and John, Finn J.D. *H.P. Lovecraft: The Complete Omnibus Collection (annotated) (2-volume set)*. Pulp-Lit Productions, 2016. Hardcover, paperback, e-book, audiobook [**ofor.us/p24** and **ofor.us/p25**].
- Burroughs, Edgar Rice. *The Lost Continent (original title: Beyond Thirty)*. Edited by Finn J.D. John. 1915. Pulp-Lit Productions, 2015. Paperback, e-book, audiobook [**ofor.us/p21**].
- Burroughs, Edgar Rice, and John, Finn J.D. *The Tarzan Duology of Edgar Rice Burroughs (annotated)*. Pulp-Lit Productions, 2015. Paperback, e-book, audiobook [**ofor.us/p23**].
- Howard, Robert E., and John, Finn J.D. *The Hour of the Dragon: Annotated Storytellers' Edition*. Pulp-Lit Productions, 2015. Paperback, e-book, audiobook [**ofor.us/p22**].
- Burroughs, Edgar Rice, and John, Finn J.D. *The John Carter Trilogy of Edgar Rice Burroughs (annotated)*. Pulp-Lit Productions, 2014. Hardcover, paperback, e-book, audiobook [**ofor. us/p20**].
- John, Finn J.D. *Wicked Portland: The Wild and Lusty Underworld of a Frontier Seaport Town*. Charleston, S.C.: The History Press, 2012. Paperback, e-book, audiobook, dedicated website (accessed through QR codes) [**wicked-portland.com**].

Articles, various publications:

- "Lynching of Innocent Man Kicked Off Vigilante Rule in Crook County." *Prineville Territory* magazine, Spring 2013.
- "Faking it: The Author as Poseur." *Etude Magazine*, Winter 2010.
- "Taking Flight: The Heroic Final Flight of Cottage Grove's Jim Wright." *Etude Magazine*, Spring 2009.

Articles, Offbeat Oregon History:

Offbeat Oregon History is a weekly syndicated column published in *McMinnville News-Register, Creswell Chronicle, McKenzie River Reflections, Cottage Grove Sentinel, Tri-County Review, Springfield Times, Redmond Spokesman, Drain Enterprise, Madras Pioneer, Dead Mountain Echo, Douglas County Mail, Daily Astorian, Clatskanie Chief, Curry Pilot, Columbia Press, Lincoln*

County Dispatch, Pendleton Record, Medford Mail-Tribune, Burns Times-Herald, Oregon Senior News and *Willamette Living Magazine.*

Offbeat Oregon columns from 2016 [ofor.us/ofor16]:
- "Oregon's Initiative and Referendum system: The real story," Dec. 25, 2016;
- "Oregon built Liberty Ships faster than the Nazis built torpedoes," Dec. 18, 2016;
- "The Oregon Electric railroad line: Ghosts of the Progressive Era," Dec. 11, 2016;
- "Oregon beach beeswax is from a 400-year-old sunken treasure ship," Dec. 4, 2016;
- "Bringing a preacher on a Prohibition liquor raid was a bad idea," Nov. 27, 2016;
- "Once Oregon's soggiest town, Valsetz is now a memory," Nov. 20, 2016;
- "'Atlantic City of the West' was swallowed up by the sea," Nov. 13, 2016;
- "In gold-rush-era Jacksonville, the bank 'robbed' you," Nov. 6, 2016;
- "'Father of Oregon Geology' once left graffiti deep in Oregon Caves," Oct. 30, 2016;
- "Bootlegger's liquor buy ended up soaking borrowed car with blood," Oct. 23, 2016;
- "How Andy Warhol 'punk'd' two Oregon colleges, and how he was caught," Oct. 16, 2016;
- "Gold Rush stagecoach driver One-Eyed Charley had an astonishing secret," Oct. 9, 2016;
- "Oregon has been home to someone since before 12,000 B.C.," Oct. 2, 2016;
- "1880s feud ended with double murder by masked assassins," Sept. 25, 2016;
- "Former Albany newsman saved Crater Lake for a national park," Sept. 18, 2016;
- "Fish wheel pilings a reminder of when Columbia swarmed with salmon," Sept. 11, 2016;
- "Did Oregon's political supervillain save the world from Nazi nukes?" Sept. 4, 2016;
- "'Graveyard of the Pacific' was not easily tamed," Aug. 28, 2016;
- "Japan's balloon bombs could have done a lot more damage," Aug. 21, 2016;
- "Highway engineer could have had Florence singing, 'It's Raining Meat,'" Aug. 14, 2016;
- "'Christmas ship' could have used some navigation help from Santa," Aug. 7, 2016;
- "Truck bombing doomed the cause of newspapers' striking unions," July 31, 2016;
- "One man's cheating heart likely cost Portland its local newspaper," July 24, 2016;
- "Supreme Court once declared slavery legal for sailors," July 17, 2016;
- "Who had motive to frame an innocent man? Everyone did," July 10, 2016;
- "In trial, prime suspect became star witness against likely innocent man," July 3, 3016;

Publications, Trade Press (continued):

- "Did brutal wartime murder end in cynical 'railroad job'?" June 26, 2016;
- "The ship that suddenly broke in half while moored at the dock," June 19, 2016;

- "For captain and crew, catastrophic shipwreck was luckiest break of their lives," June 12, 2016;
- "'Heaven's Gate' UFO cult lured away 20 Oregonians, caused statewide panic," June 5, 2016;
- "Albany's 'Queen of Fakirs' belongs in swindlers' hall of fame," May 29, 2016;
- "Southern Oregon populist leader had plans for a guerilla uprising," May 22, 2016;
- "The Jackson County Rebellion: Llewellyn Banks comes to power," May 15, 2016;
- "'Jackson County Rebellion' grew out of newspapers' fight," May 8, 2016;
- "Edward F. Lee was Oregon's first fake-viagra scammer," May 1, 2016;
- "Frontier Oregon Swindlers: The traveling medicine shows," April 24, 2016;
- "Oregon Trail medicine; or, How Not to Die of Dysentery," April 17, 2016;
- "Oregon women served as nation's first female governor, cop and voter," April 10, 2016;
- "Abigail Scott Duniway isn't the only great woman in Oregon's history," April 3, 2016;
- "Vaudeville Susie's Riot; or, How Seriously Frontier Oregon Took its Entertainment," March 27, 2016;
- "The Circuit Preacher Chronicles: The Reverend's Roadhouse Revenge," March 20, 2016;
- "The Circuit Preacher Chronicles: Shanghaiing up a flock for the Lord," March 13, 2016;
- "The Circuit Preacher Chronicles: Rev. Wells' Wild Ride," March 6, 2016;
- "Oregon lad became a founding father of Russian communism," Feb. 28, 2016;
- "Would inventor's silver steam-powered airship have worked?" Feb. 21, 2016;
- "Benton County lad became 'Nicola Tesla of Oregon,'" Feb. 14, 2016;
- "Doomed schooner's crew was locked in race against fiery death," Feb. 7, 2016;
- "Captain's refusal to leave shipwreck angered his rescuers," Jan. 31, 2016;
- "For Milwaukie gas station owner, buying bomber was wild adventure," Jan. 24, 2016;
- "Bizarre scientific 'bone wars' touched Oregon, but barely," Jan. 17, 2016;
- "Portland's 'Jitney Wars' pitted entrepreneurs against monopoly," Jan. 10, 2016;
- "Governor Charles Martin's goons were dirty but incompetent fighters," Jan. 3, 2016.

Offbeat Oregon columns from 2015 [ofor.us/ofor15]:
- "Governor Martin tried to run Oregon like an Army base," Dec. 27, 2015;
- "Oregon's own would-be Fascist dictator: Charles H. Martin," Dec. 20, 2015;

- "Collection of 'history hoarder' now a priceless treasure," Dec. 13, 2015;
- "Incompetence and a labor strike led to deadly shipwreck," Dec. 6, 2015;
- "Charity Lamb, Oregon's most misunderstood ax-murderess," Nov. 29, 2015;
- "The all-night municipal gunfight in the town of Ione," Nov. 22, 2015;
- "Monmouth's 150-year tradition of Prohibition in Oregon," Nov. 15, 2015;
- "Keeping lighthouse running was hard, and expensive," Nov. 8, 2015;
- "To get help building lighthouse, bosses had to be sneaky," Nov. 1, 2015;
- "Tillamook Lighthouse ghost greeted keeper on first night," Oct. 25, 2015;
- "Daring rescue saved 49, made skipper toast of the coast," Oct. 18, 2015;
- "A tale of two heroes of two different Civil Wars," Oct. 11, 2015;
- "Murderer shocked when 'Unwritten Law' fails him," Oct. 4, 2015;
- "'Unwritten Law' wasn't always a disastrous moral failure," Sept. 27, 2015;
- "Clean-cut 'Unwritten Law' case turned out to be sordid and complex," Sept. 20, 2015;
- "Cop's murder turned Portland against 'Unwritten Law,'" Sept. 13, 2015;
- "Private manhunt ended with jury-approved murder," Sept. 6, 2015;
- "Man hailed as hero for murdering sister's ex-lover," Aug. 30, 2015;
- "The 'Unwritten Law': A license to kill (but only for men)," Aug. 23, 2015;
- "The ones that got away: Almost-shipwrecks on the bar," Aug. 16, 2015;
- "Six picnickers were only victims of balloon bombs," Aug. 9, 2015;
- "Shark shipwreck: Navy's loss was Cannon Beach's gain," Aug. 2, 2015;
- "Schooner doomed by skipper's fear of sailors skipping," July 26, 2015;
- "Oregon's 20th-century 'gold rush': The quest for uranium," July 19, 2015;
- "Blundering robber turned out to be Joaquin Miller's son," July 12, 2015;
- "Sudden tempest caught steamship at worst possible time," July 5, 2015;
- "Rosecrans rescue was one of Coast Guard's finest hours," June 28, 2015;
- "Cursed or not, S.S. Rosecrans was unusually unlucky," June 21, 2015;
- "'Ship of Romance and Death' came to a dramatic end," June 14, 2015;
- "The small-town police chief who was executed for murder," June 7, 2015;
- "FBI's 'Most Wanted' gangster was busted in Beaverton," May 31, 2015;
- "Oregon's highest, smallest city once had its jail stolen," May 24, 2015;
- "Mount Angel Abbey owes grandeur to colorful Swiss monk," May 17, 2015;
- "Storm-tossed ships shared double date with destiny," May 10, 2015;
- "Oregon's Doolittle raiders made history in startling ways," May 3, 2015;
- "The Oregonians who flew with the Doolittle Raid over Tokyo," April 26, 2015;
- "Famous 'Doolittle Raid' had roots in Pendleton air base," April 19, 2015;
- "French sailors miraculously saved from death on the bar," April 12, 2015;
- "Pioneering historian earned recognition, but little money," April 4, 2015;
- "Legendary 'authoress' started with poetry, dime novels," March 29, 2015;
- "Civil War plotters hoped to get West Coast to secede," March 22, 2015;
- "Coast Guard 'Sand Pounders' kept Oregon Coast secure," March 15, 2015;
- "Gold dredge scheme failed — luckily for Tarzan fans," March 8, 2015;
- "Shipwrecked sailors drifted from Oregon to Puget Sound," March 1, 2015;
- "Lafe Pence's crazy plan: Move mountains down, fill up lake," Feb. 22, 2015;

Publications, Trade Press (continued):

- "Bold bandits robbed express train three miles from Roseburg," Feb. 15, 2015;
- "Cow Creek Canyon robbers weren't afraid to blow stuff up," Feb. 8, 2015;
- "When the rebel flag flew over Oregon soil," Feb. 1, 2015;
- "Oregon crooks have always enjoyed their dynamite," Jan. 25, 2015;
- "How to rob trains with dynamite: Tips from the pros," Jan. 18, 2015;
- "Dynamite used to be a regular part of Oregon life," Jan. 11, 2015;
- "Express clerk's silence foiled train robbery," Jan. 4, 2015.

Offbeat Oregon columns from 2014 [ofor.us/ofor14]:
- "Roseburg 'Champagne Riot' likely wasn't what you think," Dec. 28, 2014;
- "Oregon senator almost became President; luckily, he didn't," Dec. 21, 2014;
- "Simpson empire made Coos Bay shipbuilding Mecca," Dec. 14, 2014;
- "Free-love 'Harmonial Brotherhood' colony was a disaster," Dec. 7, 2014;
- "The father of Oregon's nursery industry's 'free-love' cult," Nov. 30, 2014;
- "Shouldn't Oregon's official language be Chinook?," Nov. 23, 2014;
- "Wreck of the steamer U.S. Grant: Baffling historical mystery," Nov. 16, 2014;
- "Nutty 1890s governor left Oregon with two Thanksgivings," Nov. 9, 2014;
- "The short, tragic story of Portland's municipal whale," Nov. 2, 2014;
- "Scholarly Albany flyer was true father of Oregon aviation," Oct. 26, 2014;
- "Offer of bonus turned out badly for owner of wrecked ship," Oct. 19, 2014;
- "Port Orford P.R. wizard managed 'secession' like a movie," Oct. 12, 2014;
- "Famous 1941 Jefferson 'secession' largely a publicity stunt," Oct. 5, 2014;
- "Oregon Indian prince was Japan's introduction to the West," Sept. 28, 2014;
- "A secret Native American prince's quest to reach Japan," Sept. 21, 2014;
- "Legendary 'Chief Bigfoot' as elusive as his hairy namesake," Sept. 14, 2014;
- "Merrill brought bikes to women; prostitutes took them away," Sept. 7, 2014;
- "Portland stunt made local aero-daredevil world famous," Aug. 31, 2014;
- "Massive war game covered Central Oregon in 1943," Aug. 24, 2014;
- "Massive steamer wrecked by future Costa Rica Navy admiral," Aug. 17, 2014;
- "Thousands of Oregonians remember replanting Tillamook Burn," Aug. 10, 2014;
- "Tillamook Burn 'blew up' with shocking speed," Aug. 3, 2014;
- "Tillamook Burn sprang from logging crew's unwise gamble," July 27, 2014;
- "Bunco Kelley: The Coyote of Portland's waterfront mythos," July 20, 2014;
- "Oregon's most notorious shanghai artist: 'Bunco' Kelley," July 13, 2014;
- "Rumors of sunken submarines: The government denies it, but ...," July 6, 2014;
- "Atlantis in the Beaver State: Underwater lost cities of Oregon," June 29, 2014;
- "Pioneer Chinese doctor was a municipal treasure in John Day," June 22, 2014;
- "Did Vortex music festival prevent riots in downtown Portland?," June 15, 2014;
- "Governor McCall expected 'Vortex I' to cost him the election," June 8, 2014;
- "Riot at PSU set the stage for 'Governor's Pot Party,'" June 1, 2014;
- "Pirates were defeated in Yaquina Bay Oyster War," May 25, 2014;
- "Portland's Pioneer Square could have been a 'crystal palace,'" May 18, 2014;

- "NASA's 'Moon Trees' have roots in an Oregon forest fire," May 11, 2014;
- "The mysterious disappearance of a schooner's entire crew," May 4, 2014;
- "Japanese shipwrecks on Oregon coast likely predate Columbus," April 27, 2014;
- "Bad batch of 'dehorn' alcohol killed 28 hobos on Skid Road," April 20, 2014;
- "Beavercreek Bomber: 'Give me $1 million or the lights go out,'" April 13, 2014;
- "Cayuse tribe's world-beating ponies are now very rare," April 6, 2014;
- "Iconic movies filmed in Oregon: Part Three, 1975-1989," March 30, 2014;
- "Iconic movies filmed in Oregon: Part Two, 1965-1975," March 23, 2014;
- "Iconic movies filmed in Oregon: Part One, 1908-1952," March 16, 2014;
- "Brutal 'Oregon Boot' made our state prison famous," March 9, 2014;
- "After logger's murder, bordello madam mysteriously vanished," March 2, 2014;
- "Hank Vaughan in middle age: The outlaw as elder statesman," Feb. 23, 2014;
- "Hank Vaughan: Becoming the West's most successful rustler," Feb. 16, 2014;
- "Legendary hell-raising rustler Hank Vaughan: The early years," Feb. 9, 2014;
- "Opium culture a long-forgotten part of the urban underworld," Feb. 2, 2014;
- "Charming gentleman by day, highway robber by night," Jan. 26, 2014;
- "Portland is home of world's only working PT boat from WWII," Jan. 19, 2014;
- "Portland's Vaudeville mayor made city famous (and infamous)," Jan 12, 2014;
- "The Oregonian once burgled a mayoral candidate's home," Jan. 5, 2014.

Offbeat Oregon columns from 2013 [ofor.us/ofor13]:
- "Wives were stripped of American citizenship at the altar," Dec. 29, 2013;
- "Bad recording technique led FBI to investigate 'Louie Louie,'" Dec. 22, 2013;
- "The game of Faro was a crooked gambler's dream," Dec. 15, 2013;
- "Taming of the Rascal: Edouard Chambreau's redemption," Dec. 8, 2013;
- "Edouard Chambreau gave a swindler's-eye view of old Oregon," Dec. 1, 2013;
- "'Blue Ruin' drove lawmakers to drink — and to Prohibition," Nov. 24, 2013;
- "Palatial riverboat was caught in a hurricane on the open sea," Nov. 17, 2013;
- "Outlaw Bill Miner's first train robbery was a fiasco," Nov. 10, 2013;
- "Was suspicious death in 'The Boneyard' really a murder?" Nov. 3, 2013;
- "Vigilantes went too far with murder of suspected rustler," Oct. 27, 2013;
- "The life and death of a gangster and his 'moll,'" Oct. 20, 2013;
- "Voice of Goofy, Bluto and Grumpy was Oregon's 'Pinto' Colvig," Oct. 13, 2013;
- "Legendary Civil War ship came to ignominious end in Coos Bay," Oct. 5, 2013;
- "The mysterious skeletons of Crater Lake National Park," Sept. 29, 2013;
- "When the 'Dark Strangler' stalked the streets of Portland," Sept. 22, 2013;
- "Train robbery turned into on-board gunfight with the law," Sept. 15, 2013;
- "1890s 'march on Washington' involved train hijackings," Sept. 8, 2013;
- "Valsetz newspaper and its editor, age 9, won nationwide fame," Sept. 1, 2013;
- "Shevlin: Oregon's wandering timber town," Aug. 25, 2013;
- "Tawdry love triangle ended in murder — and a kiss from a corpse," Aug. 18, 2013;
- "Race exclusion of early Oregon is still embarrassing today," Aug. 11, 2013;

Publications, Trade Press (continued):

- "Bootlegger's Paradise: Oregon's Prohibition adventures," Aug. 4, 2013;
- "Mob racketeers, corrupt union men battled over pinball," July 28, 2013;
- "When steamboats exploded on the upper Willamette," July 21, 2013;
- "Oregon's Harry Lane: A real hero of the First World War," July 14, 2013;
- "McCarty Gang's Oregon story: 'Bonanza' meets 'Unforgiven,'" July 7, 2013;
- "Frontier journalists settled their differences with a gunfight," June 30, 2013;
- "What really happened to D.B. Cooper? Pick a theory," June 23, 2013;
- "The Hunt for D.B. Cooper: Searching for the drop zone," June 16, 2013;
- "The deplaning of D.B. Cooper: Getting away with the loot," June 9, 2013;
- "The D.B. Cooper skyjacking legend took flight out of PDX," June 2, 2013;
- "Joseph bank robber became VP of the bank he once robbed," May 26, 2013;
- "A town's special friendship with its onetime would-be destroyer," May 18, 2013;
- "The flying Samurai who attacked Oregon," May 12, 2013;
- "Did Oregon miss a chance to catch the Zodiac Killer?" May 5, 2013;
- "Corruption, hypocrisy and the fall of the house of Klux," April 28, 2013;
- "The rise of the house of Klux: How the KKK took over the state," April 21, 2013;
- "Rise of the Ku Klux Klan in Oregon: A racist moneymaking scheme," April 14, 2013;
- "Massive 1934 Portland dock strike paralyzed the state," April 7, 2013;
- "Union squabbles were part of life on Portland waterfront," March 31, 2013;
- "Bridge-building scandal aroused fury of 1920s Portland," March 24, 2013;
- "Massive passenger liner won race against fiery death," March 17, 2013;
- "Rabies epidemic was like a war in eastern Oregon," March 10, 2013;
- "Early anti-prostitution crusade was an embarrassing fizzle," March 3, 2013;
- "A deadly maritime concert of timidity and incompetence," Feb. 24, 2013;
- "'Camp Castaway' was an inconvenient miracle," Feb. 17, 2013;
- "First public execution in Portland still surrounded with mystery," Feb. 9, 2013;
- "Mill owner's fight with city sparked anti-Japanese riot," Feb. 2, 2013;
- "Radical Wobblies found support among Oregon loggers," Jan. 27, 2013;
- "In Great War, Allies flew planes made of Oregon spruce," Jan. 20, 2013;
- "Gun-toting 'Oregon Wildcat' was America's first 'shock jock,'" Jan. 13, 2013;
- "Larry Sullivan's internationally notorious shanghaiing syndicate," Jan. 6, 2013.

Offbeat Oregon columns from 2012 [ofor.us/ofor12]:
- "Larry Sullivan: Boxer, politician, con artist, shanghai man," Dec. 30, 2012;
- "Chemawa School: An Oregon cultural treasure," Dec. 23, 2012;
- "Jim Turk: Shanghaier, swindler, drunkard, millionaire," Dec. 16, 2012;
- "Teenager's visit to Portland ended with life in prison," Dec. 9, 2012;
- "The fall of the Prineville Vigilantes," Dec. 2, 2012;
- "When the Vigilantes ruled in Prineville," Nov. 25, 2012;
- "Horrifying asylum kitchen mix-up left dozens dead," Nov. 18, 2012;
- "Courthouse Square was the site of palatial 'Hotel Portland,'" Nov. 11, 2012;

- "Boozy generosity turned the tables for the Prineville Nine that day," Nov. 4, 2012;
- "Senator John H. Mitchell: The Snidely Whiplash of Oregon," Oct. 28, 2012;
- "Long-lost Guild's Lake was once Portland's water wonderland," Oct. 21, 2012;
- "Mysterious skeletons of Oregon: If these bones could speak ...," Oct. 14, 2012;
- "Deadly weather catches Oregon by surprise when it comes," Oct. 7, 2012;
- "Auburn: A long-gone gold town's short but colorful past," Sept. 30, 2012;
- "Buck Rogers-style police boat didn't work out for Portland," Sept. 23, 2012;
- "Oregon's most famous elephant led a colorful and tragic life," Sept. 16, 2012;
- "The story of Lotus Isle, Oregon's most surreal amusement park," Sept. 9, 2012;
- "Fort Rock's legendary Reub Long could spin a wild 'tall tale,'" Sept. 2, 2012;
- "Schemers sought to seize Peter Iredale shipwreck, sell for scrap," Aug. 26, 2012;
- "Apollo 15 astronaut left a piece of Oregon lava on the moon," Aug. 19, 2012;
- "Before newspaper 'crusade,' tainted milk was killing babies," Aug. 12, 2012;
- "Long-gone dance hall hosted Chuck Berry, Johnny Cash, more," Aug. 5, 2012;
- "Rusty derelict turned out to be historic Liberty Ship lifeboat," July 29, 2012;
- "Busting out of the joint was a job for a safecracker, 100 years ago," July 22, 2012;
- "Prison break happened during 'conjugal visit' at cheap motel," July 15, 2012;
- "Quest for 'Lost Cabin Gold Mine' led to discovery of Crater Lake," July 8, 2012;
- "Crooked gambler and liquor peddler was Portland's first police chief," July 1, 2012;
- "In 1880s, salmon were the real 'most dangerous catch,'" June 24, 2012;
- "Oregon lost world's biggest log cabin in spectacular 1964 fire," June 17, 2012;
- "The mysterious demise of the S.S. South Coast: What happened?" June 10, 2012;
- "How Oregon almost lost public access to its beaches," June 3, 2012;
- "Oregon's first female lawyer: A legal Mother Teresa?" May 27, 2012;
- "Pioneering Oregon 'lady lawyer' deserved a better legacy," May 20, 2012;
- "Oregon's first female lawyer faced trial for murder of her husband," May 13, 2012;
- "'Roaring Twenties' murder mystery solved by cop's diligence," May 6, 2012;
- "Giant skeleton find recalled old legend of pirate treasure," April 29, 2012;
- "Historic mansion was once home of Portland 'starvation cult,'" April 22, 2012;
- "Oregon man's Supreme Court confirmation scotched by his wife," April 15, 2012;
- "Mass murderer honored in monument at county courthouse," April 8, 2012;
- "Mariner survived shipwreck by being trapped in the wreckage," April 1, 2012;
- "Shanghaied in Astoria: Port city was once a perilous place," March 25, 2012;
- "'Oregon's Outback' was a real moonshiner's paradise in the '20s," March 18, 2012;
- "Postwar Portland turned away Nat 'King' Cole, Billie Holiday," March 11, 2012;
- "Cruise-ship skipper wasn't first to 'fall into a lifeboat,'" March 4, 2012;
- "Incompetent opium smugglers had friends in high places," Feb. 25, 2012;

Publications, Trade Press (continued):

- "First seaworthy log raft helped Oregon build city of San Diego," Feb. 19, 2012;
- "Fog made the difference between a reprimand and a medal," Feb. 12, 2012;
- "Homesteader's plan to get extra land involved bigamy, murder," Feb. 5, 2012;
- "Forty-day debauch made Oregon legislature nationally notorious," Jan. 29, 2012;
- "Coast Guard catastrophe sprang from bad boat design," Jan. 22, 2012;
- "Coast Guard's worst Columbia disaster started as routine rescue," Jan. 15, 2012;
- "Tangent City Hall office cat was the city's landlord," Jan. 8, 2012;
- "Oregon City was home of world's first electric power grid," Jan. 1, 2012.

Offbeat Oregon columns from 2011 [ofor.us/ofor11]:
- "Dory fisherman rescues stranded sailors — from Coast Guard boat," Dec. 25, 2011;
- "'Voice of Looney Toons' was the terror of his Portland high school," Dec. 18, 2011;
- "The Port Orford Meteorite: Was it all a big hoax?" Dec. 11, 2011;
- "Missing gold suggests something sinister in shipwreck mystery," Dec. 4, 2011;
- "Portland was the scene of Sammy Davis Jr.'s big break," Nov. 28, 2011;
- "'Black sheep of the Union army' was Oregon's last Civil War veteran," Nov. 21, 2011;
- "Oregon's distinctive bridge style is Conde McCullough's legacy," Nov. 14, 2011;
- "Captain's quick decision saved hundreds from a fiery death," Nov. 7, 2011;
- "Steamboat monopoly's clever coup ended up costing them plenty," Oct. 31, 2011;
- "They laughed at Captain Scott's ugly little riverboat ... until ...," Oct. 24, 2011;
- "For one Oregon slave, Civil War didn't end bondage," Oct. 17, 2011;
- "Rascally sea-captain was like a 19th-century Han Solo," Oct. 10, 2011;
- "Aurora Colony showcased the best of the American Utopian movement," Oct. 3, 2011;
- "Oregon embraced Carnegie Libraries like no other state," Sept. 26, 2011;
- "Astoria man set out to do something for his wife, invented cable TV," Sept. 19, 2011;
- "'Professor' Ray V.B. Jackson: Central Oregon's 'Angel of Death,'" Sept. 12, 2011;
- "Schoolteacher Ray Jackson of Silver Lake may have been a serial killer," Sept. 4, 2011;
- "Ship sailed across two miles of sandy beach, relaunched itself," Aug. 28, 2011;
- "First youth symphony in U.S. came out of Oregon's high desert," Aug. 21, 2011;
- "Vaudeville's famous 'Klondike Kate' became a Central Oregon legend," Aug. 14, 2011;
- "Space-age whalers helped grow fur coats, put a man on the moon," Aug. 7, 2011;

- "Shipwreck ends Astoria's bid to be 'Nantucket of the West Coast,'" Aug. 7, 2011;
- "In marshal's saloon, drinks were on Prohibitionist governor West," July 31, 2011;
- "Life of Sacagawea's mountain-man son a tantalizing mystery," July 25, 2011;
- "Mariner's dream predicted shipmates' deaths with eerie precision," July 17, 2011;
- "Little-known hero of Silver Lake fire died saving dozens of lives," July 10, 2011;
- "Wreck of the Glenesslin: Insurance fraud, or drunken incompetence?" July 3, 2011;
- "Gold-field bandits' stolen loot still hasn't been found," June 26, 2011;
- "Tired of watching mariners die, lighthouse keeper started rescue service," June 19, 2011;
- "Legendary Oregon wrestler pinned by heavyweight real-estate dream," June 12, 2011;
- "Story of 'nudist church' in Corvallis ended in murder, suicide, insanity," June 5, 2011;
- "The real story of the 'nudist church' in Corvallis: How it began," May 29, 2011;
- "Blimps were first line of defense against Japanese subs, balloon bombs," May 21, 2011;
- "Crew of shipwrecked schooner rescued — by a railroad train," May 14, 2011;
- "'Hermit of the Craggies' went from acorns and roots to prison food," May 7, 2011;
- "Coast Guard rescued ship — for Stalin's most notorious gulag," May 1, 2011;
- "Gallon House covered bridge: Ground Zero in Oregon's battle over booze," April 24, 2011;
- "Amateur pirates' bumbling scheme didn't work out as they'd planned," April 17, 2011;
- "Only sitting U.S. Senator killed in battle was from Oregon ... sort of," April 10, 2011;
- "Bungling burglars skunked in Corvallis courthouse job," April 3, 2011;
- "Oregon had first female governor in U.S. history — for one weekend," March 27, 2011;
- "Eugene woman first female VP candidate to get Electoral College vote," March 27, 2011;
- "Harney County rancher saved pioneer Oregon aviator's life," March 19, 2011;
- "Did Buddhist monk from China 'discover' Oregon 1,600 years ago?" March 13, 2011;
- "Chinese gold smuggler saved woman and her baby, then vanished," March 5, 2011;
- "Tiny home-built schooner 'Morning Star' saved Tillamook settlers," Feb. 27, 2011;
- "When dynamite truck blew up Roseburg, it looked like nuclear war," Feb. 20, 2011;

Publications, Trade Press (continued):

- "Shipwrecked fur traders walked from Oregon Coast to Louisiana," Feb. 13, 2011;
- "Little remains of back-woods luxury spa at Wilhoit Springs Park," Feb. 6, 2011;
- "Japanese submarine I-25 blasted its way into Oregon history — twice," Jan. 30, 2011;
- "Vanport houses floated like life rafts, helped many survive the flood," Jan. 23, 2011;
- "Oregon backcountry rich in legends of buried treasure and robbers' loot," Jan. 16, 2011;
- "Little boy somehow knew mom and aunt were drowning in shipwreck," Jan. 9, 2011;
- "Bobbie the Wonder Dog's 2,500-mile odyssey put Silverton on the map," Jan. 2, 2011.

Offbeat Oregon columns from 2010 [ofor.us/ofor10]:

- "Caught rescuing shipwrecked sailors, rumrunners sent to prison anyway," Dec. 27, 2010;
- "Depoe Bay, the world's smallest harbor, used to be even smaller," Dec. 20, 2010;
- "America's first 'rest area' had marble walls, crowns scenic highway," Dec. 13, 2010;
- "Temperance crusaders showed saloon keeper a real 'bar fight,'" Dec. 5, 2010;
- "Did this tiny, soggy, scary road save Oregon's public beaches?" Nov. 28, 2010;
- "Town of Bandon destroyed by its founder's favorite garden shrub," Nov. 21, 2010;
- "Last geyser in Pacific Northwest has gone still in Lakeview," Nov. 14, 2010;
- "Portland Trail Blazers' fate hung on extra-long bathroom break," Nov. 7, 2010;
- "Mountain ghost town home of Oregon's greatest mining swindle," Nov. 1, 2010;
- "Family camped unnoticed in downtown Portland for years," Oct. 24, 2010;
- "Fossil Lake: Oregon's answer to the LaBrea Tar Pits," Oct. 17, 2010;

- "Oregon City is home of America's steepest street — it runs straight up," Oct. 10, 2010;
- "Marcus Whitman wanted to 'save' Oregon, but not from British," Oct. 3, 2010;
- "Why legendary Old West lawman Virgil Earp is buried in Oregon," Sept. 27, 2010;
- "Cattlemen-Sheepmen wars had more than 10,000 wooly casualties," Sept. 20, 2010;
- "'Guns of August' blasted Nature Man's quest to prove he wasn't a fraud," Sept. 13. 2010;
- "Columbia was a wild, dangerous place once — especially Celilo Falls," Sept. 6, 2010;

- "When banks closed, North Bend minted its own money out of wood," Aug. 29, 2010;
- "The legendary Spanish gold of Neahkahnie Mountain," Aug. 22, 2010;
- "West Coast's first female doctor lived in Oregon," Aug. 15, 2010;
- "Without Astorians' 'failure,' Oregon would be part of Canada, eh?" Aug. 8, 2010;
- "Oregon state governor to President of the United States: 'Drop dead,'" Aug. 1, 2010;
- "West's first floating bordello was in Portland's Willamette River," July 26, 2010;
- "Wagon train to Oregon was led by a dead man," July 19, 2010;
- "Harry Tracy, the Last Desperado, gunned down after bloody jailbreak," July 12, 2010;
- "'Flumgudgeon Gazette,' Oregon's first newspaper, was hand-written," July 5, 2010;
- "Lewis and Clark left trail of heavy-metal laxatives across the country," June 29, 2010;
- "Portland was the 'Shanghai capital of the world' in the 1890s," June 21, 2010;
- "Lincoln City's D River is part-time holder of a world record ... sort of," June 14, 2010;
- "Pioneer preacher was more than Legislature bargained for," June 6, 2010;
- "Rajneeshpuram: Did it almost become an Oregon Jonestown?" May 30, 2010;
- "Rajneeshpuram: The collapse of the Bhagwan's city," May 23, 2010;
- "Rajneeshpuram: Oregon's 'red scare' featured Rolls-Royces," May 16, 2010;
- "Rajneeshpuram, Oregon's most infamous ashram: The backstory," May 9, 2010;
- "Oregon astronauts made history in good and not-so-good ways," May 2, 2010;
- "Camp Adair, state's second-largest city, built in six months," April 24, 2010;
- "Flash flood in Oregon in 1903 was nation's deadliest," April 18, 2010;
- "Boiler Bay named for fiery, spectacular 1910 shipwreck," April 11, 2010;
- "Wolf Creek Tavern was Jack London's writing retreat," April 4, 2010;
- "Is Oregon's crystal cave just a legend? Well ...," March 28, 2010;
- "Old excursion train is now a new bike path," March 21, 2010;
- "Mohawk Valley debated school with dynamite," March 14, 2010;
- "Lure of the sea brought potatoes to Oregon," March 6, 2010;
- "Oregon Vortex: 80 years of keeping 'em guessing," Feb. 28, 2010;
- "Dispute over reservation land lasted 101 years," Feb. 21, 2010;
- "Bits of Hollywood train wreck still in Row River," Feb. 14, 2010;
- "For pioneer family, highway robbers were lifesavers," Feb. 7, 2010;
- "Underground city found in Pendleton potholes," Jan. 31, 2010;
- "Gold country legend: The solid-gold snuff can," Jan. 25, 2010;
- "Biggest meteorite in U.S. found in West Linn," Jan. 18, 2010;
- "Bing cherry has roots on Oregon Trail," Jan. 11, 2010;
- "Timberline Lodge could have been a skyscraper," Jan. 3, 2010.

Publications, Trade Press (continued):

Offbeat Oregon columns from 2008 and 2009 [ofor.us/ofor09]:

- "Yaquina ghost story is pure fiction ... or is it?" Dec. 27, 2009;
- "Grande Ronde Valley: Eden, used-oxen dealership," Dec. 21, 2009;
- "Pixieland: Memories of an edgy amusement park," Dec. 14, 2009;
- "Lightship had to go cross-country to reach sea," Dec. 7, 2009;
- "BLM and Straub stopped plan for highway on beach," Nov. 15, 2009;
- "Oregon had inside track on California gold rush," Nov. 8, 2009;
- "Martial law declared in bawdy mining town," Nov. 5, 2009;
- "Have you heard of Marie Dorion?" Oct. 29, 2009;
- "Early naturalist thwarted by hungry, thirsty fellow travelers," Oct. 21, 2009;
- "Nation's only wheelchair-accessible tidepools," Oct. 6, 2009;
- "Pioneer governor was made of tough stuff," Oct. 1, 2009;
- "Corvallis's cattle-powered riverboat experiment," Sept. 30, 2009;
- "Ice skating on Cottage Grove Lake?" Sept. 23, 2009;
- "The scandalous secret of One-Eyed Charley," Sept. 23, 2009;
- "Bonus Army of 1932 started in Portland," Sept. 19, 2009;
- "When Portland floods, folks raise the sidewalks," Sept. 16, 2009;
- "Jacksonville: Where gold was as cheap as salt," Sept. 10, 2009;
- "Mount Hood celebrated statehood with fireworks," Sept. 6, 2009;
- "AWS spotted few enemies, but saved many friends," Sept. 3, 2009;
- "Graveyard of Oregon Trail still said to be haunted," Aug. 24, 2009;
- "Ghost stories still haunt century-old tavern," Aug. 23, 2009;
- "Hank Vaughan's most profitable 'gunfight,'" Aug. 17, 2009;
- "Portland man woke up during his wake," Aug. 13, 2009;
- "14,000-year-old fossilized people poop?" Aug. 2, 2009;
- "Man paddled over Silver Falls and survived," July 27, 2009;
- "Lighthouse built 3 weeks too late for 16 sailors," July 22, 2009;
- "Did Japan's wartime balloon bombs start the 1945 Tillamook Burn?" July 15, 2009;
- "Unexploded WWII bomb rode in glovebox," July 10, 2009;
- "Ashland Shakespeare plays beat out boxing event," July 8, 2009;
- "Florence's famous Exploding Whale," July 2, 2009;
- "Did Sir Francis Drake summer in Whale Cove?" June 8, 2009;
- "Mule-powered railroad was a desperate gambit," May 31, 2009;
- "The Swine Flu: Is it deja vu?" Msay 24, 2009;
- "Oregon helped Hoover prevent mass starvation," May 21, 2009;
- "Oregon freeways were the envy of the West," May 10, 2009;
- "Granite: An old mining town that's almost a ghost," May 5, 2009;
- "The President from Oregon who fed millions," May 3, 2009;
- "Snubbed by railroad, Prineville built its own," May 3, 2009;
- "Farmer from Oregon started California's gold rush," April 26, 2009;
- "No one has ever found legendary lost gold mine," April 19, 2009;
- "This was the lake that wasn't, but then was," April 12, 2009;

- "13 was unlucky number in Oregon train robbery," April 6, 2009;
- "Liberty ships: Building 'em faster than Hitler could sink 'em," April 2, 2009;
- "Oregon Electric railroad line: State's past — and future?" March 22, 2009;
- "Love Crater Lake? Thank an Albany newspaperman," March 22, 2009;
- "Coming soon to a beach near you: 350-year-old beeswax," March 18, 2009;
- "Valsetz: Company town was soggy, but home," March 7, 2009;
- "The Oregon town that fell into the sea," Feb. 25, 2009;
- "A pioneer scientist's graffiti in a cave," Feb. 19, 2009;
- "Oregon's Centennial: The $19 million party," Feb. 11, 2009;
- "Oregon art students got 'punk'd' by Andy Warhol & Co.," Feb. 1, 2009;
- "Pioneer Chinese doctor was a municipal treasure in John Day," Feb. 5, 2009;
- "Fish wheels back in service — to save fish?" Dec. 3, 2008;
- "Did Bonneville Dam win World War II?" Oct. 1, 2008.

Publications, Electronic and New Media:

Podcasts:
- Offbeat Oregon History podcast [**ofor.us/itunes** or **ofor.us/pcst**]. Thrice-weekly podcast derived from the archives of the Offbeat Oregon History newspaper column. Launched December 2011. Averages roughly 1,000 downloads per episode.
- Friederich Wilhelm von Junzt Library of Forgotten Worlds [**ofor.us/vj-itunes** or **vj-pcst**]. Weekly alternate-reality podcast centered around readings of weird-fiction short stories, inspired by H.P. Lovecraft and Welcome to Night Vale. Launched in June 2014.

RSS feeds (XML):
- Offbeat Oregon History Newsfeed [**ofor.us/t**]. Weekly RSS feed of fresh Offbeat Oregon columns for subscribers using newsreaders.

Blogs:
- Offbeat Oregon History [**offbeatoregon.com**]. Browsable and searchable collection of all previously published Offbeat Oregon History newspaper columns (424 as of Jan. 1, 2017), organized by date of first publication. (Site hand-coded in HTML and CSS; no CMS system in use)

Websites and social media pages:
- **finnjohn.com**. Central hub page for all on-line franchises.
- **offbeatoregon.com**. Website functions as sub-hub for the Offbeat Oregon History franchise, including the blog content as well as links out to social-media assets (listed below). Launched 2008; currently averages 45,000 unique visits per month.
- **facebook.com/ofor.OregonHistory**: 4,300 page likes as of Jan. 1, 2017.
- **twitter.com/offbeatoregon**. 880 followers as of Jan. 1, 2017.
- **von-junzt.org**. Website functions as a sub-hub for the Friederich Wilhelm von Junzt Library of Forgotten Worlds franchise.
- **wicked-portland.com**: Support site for *Wicked Portland: The Wild and Lusty Underworld of a Frontier Seaport Town.*

Media enterprises:

Pulp-Lit Productions (2014-present):
> Title: Principal Creative. A publishing house that produces annotated collections of the works of classic pulp writers such as Edgar Rice Burroughs and H.P. Lovecraft in audiobook, e-book, paperback and hardcover editions, as well as reprints of hard-to-find pre-war pulp and popular fiction novels. The audiobook versions of these books are the primary focus, with exclusive distribution through Audible.com. **[pulp-lit.com]**

Travelin' Magazine (1998-2000):
> Title: Editor and Publisher. Bi-monthly consumer magazine, distributed by subscription and on newsstands, about exploring the back roads and by-ways of the American West. Now defunct.

The Real Estate Book of Eugene/Springfield (1995-1999):
> Title: Associate Publisher. Monthly real-estate advertising publication distributed free in Lane County, Ore.

Presentations and Public Lectures:

Presentations:
- Presentation, "The Mysterious Portland Shanghaiing Scene, 1849-1928," at Corvallis Genealogical Society meeting, Feb. 13, 2016;
- Presentation, "Herbert Hoover's Tracks in Oregon," at the Modern Travelers Club in Albany, Dec. 14, 2015;
- Multimedia presentation, "The Almost-President from Oregon: Gov. Joseph Lane and the Plan to Outfox Lincoln," at the McMinnville City Club, Oct. 13, 2015;
- Presentation, "Building Your Own Personal Broadcasting Empire," at Intercollegiate Broadcasting System symposium at KBVR studios at Oregon State University, Oct. 10, 2015;
- Multimedia presentation, "Legends and mysteries of Crater Lake," at Albany Historical Museum, Oct. 22, 2014;
- Presentation, "Herbert Hoover and the Commission for Relief in Belgium," at McMinnville Kiwanis Club, Sept. 5, 2013;
- Convention keynote address, "Wicked Politics in 1800s Portland," at the Oregon Mensa Regional Gathering in Portland, May 11, 2013;
- Kickoff speech, "Writing for Radio," at Northwest College Radio Conference at KBVR studios at Oregon State University, April 13, 2013;
- Panel discussion, "Election Campaign Ads," at League of Women Voters event at Corvallis Public Library, Sept. 18, 2012 (with Prof. Bill Loges and OPB reporter Chris Lehman);

Public lectures:
- Public lecture, "Rattling the Skeletons in Oregon's Closet," at Columbia Gorge Discovery Center & Museum, April 22, 2016;
- Public lecture, "Bootlegger's Paradise: Prohibition Adventures in Oregon," at Oregon Museum of Natural and Cultural History's "Ideas On Tap" lecture series, April 6, 2016;

- Public lecture/multimedia history show, "Wicked Politics in 1800s Portland," Willamette University, Sept. 7, 2012;
- Public lecture, "Oregon History's Secrets," at OASIS Center in Eugene, Nov. 17, 2010;
- Public lecture, "Offbeat Lane County History," at Lane County Historical Museum, Eugene, March 4, 2010;
- Panel discussion, "Community Journalism," Society of Professional Journalists Writing Workshop, Eugene, Feb. 9, 2002 (with Rob Priewe of Corvallis Gazette-Times and Dan Spatz of The Dalles Chronicle)
- Public lecture/multimedia history show series, "Stumptown Stories": Monthly series presented in bars by the Stumptown Storytellers, a troupe of irreverent pop historians including public historian Joe Streckert, author Heather Arndt Anderson, author J.B. Fisher and podcaster Doug Kenck-Crispin [**stumptownstories.org**]. Topics:
  - "Swindler's Paradise: Oregon in the Golden Age of Patent Medicine," Sept. 13, 2016;
  - "The FBI's Most Wanted: Oregon history's baddest bad guys," Aug. 9, 2016;
  - "Danford Balch: Father of the Year for 1858," June 14, 2016;
  - "Opium smuggling in 1890s Portland," Jan. 12, 2016;
  - "Portland's Murderous Melodrama of Christmastime 1907," Dec. 8, 2015;
  - "Lafe Pence, Mover of Mountains, and his Crazy Guild's Lake Scheme," Nov. 10, 2015;
  - "Happy Labor Day from Shaghaiers Local 151, Portland; L. Sullivan, President," Sept. 8, 2015;
  - "The Oregon Boot, and The Day the Joint Got Jacked," July 14, 2015;
  - "The Lamest, Most Pathetic Attempt at a Jailbreak Ever Undertaken with the Help of Three Sticks of Dynamite," June 9, 2015;
  - "The Holy Rollers (Bride of Christ Church): Sex, naked ladies, tar and feathers, murder, suicide, and madness — Oregon style," April 13, 2015;
  - "Oregon's worst politician EVER," Feb. 9, 2015;
  - "Sylvester Pennoyer: Oregon's Father of Thanksgiving," Nov. 10, 2014;
  - "The KKK and Portland's bridge scandal," Sept. 8, 2014;
  - "Pioneer Courthouse Square: Three Portland Icons," June 5, 2014;
  - "Portland's Tawdriest Love Triangle," May 8, 2014;
  - "Murder on the Oregon Express," March 4, 2014;
  - "Opium Smuggling in Old Portland," Feb. 4, 2014;
  - "Bootlegging the Oregon Way: The Volstead years," Jan. 7, 2014;
  - "How we Almost Lost the Peter Iredale to a Crooked Scrap-Metal Man," Jan. 21, 2014;
  - "Bootlegging the Oregon way: Adventure, romance, comedy and tragedy in Oregon's second-oldest profession," Dec. 2, 2013;
  - "Embezzler, Philanderer, Racketeer, Senator," Nov. 4, 2013;
  - "The Man with the Hook Kills in Portland," Oct. 31, 2013;
  - "Mysterious Skeletons of Oregon History," Oct. 1, 2013;
  - "Weird Cults of Old Oregon," Sept. 3, 2013;
  - "The Ku Klux Klan in 1920s Oregon," Aug. 6, 2013;

Presentations and Public Lectures (continued):

- "When Masked Outlaw Riders Ruled Central Oregon: The Rise and Fall of the Prineville Vigilantes," July 2, 2013;
- "Senator John H. Mitchell: Oregon's Own Snidely Whiplash," June 4, 2013;
- "Smooth-Moving Bad Guys of Oregon History," May 7, 2013;
- "Shipwrecks of Oregon II," Feb. 5, 2013;
- "Shipwrecks of Oregon I," Nov. 6, 2012;
- "Top 5 Most Delicious Political Swindles of Old Oregon," Sept. 11, 2012.

Media appearances:

Terrestrial radio:
- KPNW AM 1120 Radio's "Wake Up Call" show (Eugene, OR): Discussed the Meadors Gang and Bill Miner train robberies, Nov. 29, 2016;
- KPNW AM 1120 Radio's "Wake Up Call" show (Eugene, OR): Discussed Baldwin v. Robertson, the 1895 Supreme Court decision that legalized slavery for sailors, Nov. 1, 2016;
- KPNW AM 1120 Radio's "Wake Up Call" show (Eugene, OR): Discussed some of the most audacious swindlers of Oregon history, Oct. 10, 2016;
- KPNW AM 1120 Radio's "Wake Up Call" show (Eugene, OR): Discussed old circuit-riding preachers in frontier Oregon, Sept. 8, 2016;
- KPNW AM 1120 Radio's "Wake Up Call" show (Eugene, OR): Discussed Thomas B. Slate and his steam-powered airship (1928), Aug. 5, 2016;
- The Travel Channel, Mysteries at the National Parks: Discussed the mysterious deaths at Crater Lake National Park on location for an upcoming Season Two episode, May 20, 2016;
- KPNW AM 1120 Radio's "Wake Up Call" show (Eugene, OR): Discussed "The Unwritten Law" in 1890s Oregon, March 22, 2016;
- KPNW AM 1120 Radio's "Wake Up Call" show (Eugene, OR): Discussed the 1904 "Bride of Christ" cult, Sept. 16, 2015;
- KPNW AM 1120 Radio's "Wake Up Call" show (Eugene, OR): Discussed the use of dynamite in Mohawk Valley school district negotiations in 1895, Aug. 19, 2015;

Television:
- The Travel Channel, *Mysteries at the Museum*: Discussed "moon trees" in the OSU library for an upcoming Season 12 episode, Nov. 10, 2016;
- The Travel Channel, *Mysteries at the National Parks*: Discussed the mysterious deaths at Crater Lake National Park on location for an upcoming episode, May 20, 2016;
- The Travel Channel, *Mysteries at the Museum*: Discussed Tusko the Elephant and the 1914 botched train robbery of the Meadors Gang for two Season 10 episodes, Sept. 2, 2015 [ofor.us/tv-mm105];
- Oregon Public Broadcasting, *Oregon Experience*: Discussed train robberies of Oregon history for "Murder on the Southern Pacific" episode (Season 9), May 4, 2015 [ofor.us/tv-oe94];

Newspapers:

- *McMinnville News-Register*: "The Oregon you never knew," by Karl Klooster (profile story), July 7, 2012.

Podcasts (besides my own):

- *Kick Ass Oregon History* podcast: Discussed the shanghaiing of sailors in 1890s Portland with Doug Kenck-Crispin for "Shanghaied in Portland!" episode (Season 5), Aug. 15, 2012 [ofor.us/kaoh52];

IV

SERVICE.

Service to Oregon State University:
- Currently serve as faculty adviser for OSU Novelists Club;
- Served as a marshal at Commencement in June of 2013, 2014, 2015 and 2016;
- Reviewed book proposal for Oregon State University Press. Subject: "Oregon History Comics" proposal by Sarah Mirk, 2013;
- Served on hiring committee for Student Media Journalism Adviser position, May 2014.
- Coordinated the drafting and collaborative fine-tuning of New Media Communications writing standards for purposes of teaching evaluation.

Service to profession:
- Vice-president, Society of Professional Journalists Greater Oregon Chapter board of directors, 2002-2004;
- Organizer and presenter, Society of Professional Journalists Training Day, Corvallis, Oregon. A day-long series of seminars on various topics presented by professional journalists. March 21, 2004;
- Member, Oregon Historical Society;
- Member, Museum of Natural and Cultural History, University of Oregon;
- Member, Willamette Writers.

V

AWARDS.

Journalism awards and honors:
- Society of Professional Journalists Northwest Region Daily Newspaper Contest:
  - 2005: Long feature: First place;
  - 2004: Food, fashion and home: Third place.
- Society of Professional Journalists Greater Oregon Chapter Non-Daily Contest:
  - 2003: Editorial writing: first place;
  - 2002: Personalities feature writing: first place; news feature writing: first place; spot news coverage: second place; Page One design: third place;
  - 2001: Business feature: first place.
- Oregon Newspaper Publishers Association Better Newspapers Contest:
  - 2006: General Excellence: third place; Page One design: honorable mention;
  - 2005: "Silk Purse" story: honorable mention;
  - 2003: Enterprise reporting: first place; general excellence: second place; Page One design: second place; editorial writing: third place;
  - 2002: Enterprise reporting: first place and third place (two awards); business reporting: first place; spot news: second place; general feature: second place; editorial writing: third place;
  - 2001: Best writing: second place; Page One design: second place; spot news: second place and third place (two awards); enterprise reporting: second place.

CONTACT INFO.

Thank you for taking time out of your day to explore my curriculum vitae. I hope that it has answered all your questions and provided you with any and all information you needed. Should it fall short of doing so, I hope you won't hesitate to contact me with any questions. Also, if you should find yourself in the Corvallis area with time for a cup of coffee, be sure and look me up.

Full contact information:

At Oregon State University:
New Media Communications
Suite 30, Margaret C. Snell Hall
2150 Southwest Jefferson Way
Corvallis, OR 97331
541.737.1492
finn.john@oregonstate.edu

At Pulp-Lit Productions:
2323 Northwest Monroe Street
Post Office Box 77
Corvallis, OR 97339
978.785.7548
finn@pulp-lit.com

At home:
27013 Northwest Sulphur Springs Road
Corvallis, OR 97330
541.357.2222
finn@finnjohn.com

www.ingramcontent.com/pod-product-compliance
Lightning Source LLC
Chambersburg PA
CBHW061959090426
42811CB00006B/989